DIMITRI HOUSE STORIES

by

FRAN MORSE

COSMOGRAPHIA BOOKS

ROCHESTER, NEW YORK

For permission to reprint portions of this book, or to order a review copy, contact:

Cosmographia Books
c/o Aurora Center for Spiritual and Creative Arts
11 N. Goodman, Suite 24
Rochester, New York 14607
Email: editor@cosmographiabooks.com

The author has tried to recreate the events, locales, and conversations in this book from her memories of them. In order to maintain their anonymity, in some instances she has changed the names of individuals, places, identifying characteristics occupations and places of residence.

Cover Design by Betsy Alvarez
Cover Photos by Kate Melton
Author Photo by Gene Renner

ISBN-13: 978-0692539620 (Cosmographia Books)
ISBN-10: 069253962X

DEDICATION

Everyone has a story that, when told, opens a window into their life.
With much gratitude, I dedicate this book to those whose stories are
told here, and also to the many others whose stories remain only in
my heart. Thank you.

Acknowledgements

I would like to thank the many people who encouraged and supported me to write my stories down, to those who read them or listened to me read them, to those who offered comments and suggestions, and to all those who believed in the possibility of this simple book.

To Nina Alvarez, Cosmographia Books Publisher, who three years ago gave me the confidence to stay on my journey and who edited and published this book.

To the rest of the Cosmographia team: Carolyn Birrittella, Betsy Alvarez, and Audrey Odhner.

To the talented photographers Kate Melton and Gene Renner.

To Dimitri House, Writers & Books, and Community Christian Church in Rochester, NY.

To Sam Goodson, although our connection was brief, who encouraged me and shared in my enthusiasm to stay with it.

To both my sons, Mark and Eric, who encouraged me to just do it and stayed on me until I did.

To God, the Divine Source in my life, whose constant presence was sensed in each encounter, stirring me to write this book.

Most of all, I thank each person whose story I wrote for inviting me into their lives.

STORIES

INTRODUCTION

WHEN YOU WALK DOWN THE STREET and you see someone who's homeless, that's a life, that's a story.

The first story I ever wrote was Byron's. I felt God's presence when I met him and right up to the day we buried him. It felt like holy work I was privileged to be a part of. It was in my heart, but it was also jumbled in my head and I never thought, "Well jeez, I'm going to sit down and I'm going to write a story." But two days after the funeral, I just needed to sit down and get it out of my head.

Then as I had experiences with other people, and I started to write things down, I was okay. I could be okay. But I kept the stories in the bottom of my file cabinet.

Occasionally I had the opportunity to do a gospel reading at Corpus Christi Church in Rochester, New York. Sometimes I would think of a person from Dimitri and then write the story, and other times I would read the gospel and recognize it in a story I'd already written. I saw the gospel in my day-to-day interactions and worked through some of my most moving experiences by writing them down. The stories would just spill out of me. It was a way to work out what I felt and witnessed.

Now I see how these stories can honor the people of Dimitri House and I am happy to be able to share them with the larger community.

The people you will meet in these stories are the men and women I met while working at Dimitri House. Dimitri House is a small nonprofit agency that attends to the needs of the poor and homeless of the Rochester community. I hope that when people read their stories, they realize that a homeless person is not just a homeless person. They had a life, they had a family.

The chapters in the book span 1991 to 2012. I changed the names of some of the people to protect their privacy. Some others, those who have passed away, I have left with their original names as a testament to their memory.

BYRON

I REMEMBER WELL THE DAY I FIRST MET BYRON. It was a hot, sticky, summer morning. I was in the kitchen getting a cup of coffee when the doorbell rang. Though it was early, I thought it might be one of the volunteers.

When I opened the door, there stood a young man with such horrific scars on his face, arms, and hands that I had to look away and catch my breath. His eyelids were tightly stretched over his sad, brown eyes, both ears were practically missing, and very little was left of his nose. I composed myself and awkwardly said, "Hi—can I help you?"

"Hi, my name is Byron. Can I take a shower?"

I invited him in and offered him a cup a coffee. He was homeless and an alcoholic. He told me, "You'd drink too, if you looked like this."

He had been a musician in the Boston area and he explained that four years ago he survived a house fire. He played keyboards and said he was damn good. "But then, that's history, so . . . I drink."

"I'd like to take a shower," he repeated. "If I can. My sweat glands were destroyed from the fire and in the summer I need to take cool showers to deal with the heat. In the winter my skin cracks so bad, it bleeds. So can I take a shower, please?"

I gathered some things for him: a towel, washcloth, underwear, socks, and hygiene products. He disappeared into the bathroom and reappeared twenty minutes later looking refreshed and smelling clean. "Man, that was great. I feel human again."

We talked for a while more, and then for the next couple of weeks he would stop by for a shower and chitchat. He began to open up to the other guests and even made some friends, telling of his adventures from when he was in his rock band. "The girls were all over me!" I'd hear him say.

He stopped in one morning to tell me that he had found an apartment. He was getting some furniture from a friend and we gave him some dishes and pots and pans. He was so excited and said he was ready to start over.

The last time I saw Byron, he was crossing Monroe Avenue. Two days later, I received a phone call from the coroner's office inquiring about "a Byron Swift."

"He was dead—found in a room off Alexander Street— been there a couple of days. No family. A card with your name and phone number was found in his room. The county will bury him."

I remember thinking, "But I just saw him! He was feeling good about himself, stopping by Dimitri House often, feeling like he belonged. He's dead?"

The funeral home in the neighborhood prepared Byron's body for burial and Corpus Christi Church had a funeral for him at a Thursday night mass. Thursday night masses at Corpus Christi were different: informal, welcoming, nontraditional. People who attended were invited up on the altar to be a part of the celebration of the Eucharist. Reaching out, serving the poor, sheltering the homeless were familiar themes of the homilies, so it seemed fitting that Byron's funeral would be celebrated at a Thursday night mass.

The priest at Corpus Christi did the eulogy and talked about how Byron would occasionally come to weekday noon mass and when mass was over, he would ask if he could play the piano. As he played, he would be transported. He loved music and he loved to play. It was the one time when he felt normal. Not many at the funeral knew Byron, but many tears were shed and he was given quite a going home celebration.

The burial was scheduled for the following day. Byron's casket wasn't much more than a plywood box covered in light blue material: a "welfare casket." I'd never seen anything like it. The day was hot and humid and there were just five of us there to say goodbye. When the hearse pulled up near the readied grave, the funeral director motioned us over. "Two of you on either side of the casket, and Father, I'll put you at the head to lead the way."

As we carried Byron to his resting place, a tall man came from out of nowhere and began to play "Danny Boy." He apparently knew Bryon from the streets. The sound of that solitary flute seemed to fill the air and drown out the nearby traffic. The priest made the Sign of the Cross and began the final blessing.

"Byron, may the angels lead you into paradise. May the martyrs greet you at your arrival and lead you into the holy city, Jerusalem. And may God hold you close until we meet again."

A warm breeze kicked up and we looked at each other and smiled. I believe we all were thinking the same thing: "Fly free now, Byron, and be at peace."

LAWRENCE

EVERYTHING LAWRENCE KNEW, he learned from his father. As a child he was always by his father's side, helping him with yard work, watching his hands as they carved and shaped woodworking projects, always deeply attentive and soaking up every ounce of his dad's attention. The bond they shared was deep and profound.

When Lawrence was eleven years old, his father died suddenly of a heart attack. Lawrence was devastated; his whole world changed in an instant. "I had to be the dad now," Lawrence would say. It was the only way he knew to adjust to his new reality—to become the man, the father of the house.

He tried desperately to fill his father's shoes, to be the provider, the strength, and the disciplinarian. But his father's death impacted Lawrence more than he knew, and being a man for his mother and younger sister, coupled with his grief, was too much for the young boy to manage. In his anguish, Lawrence became angry, volatile, unpredictable. Soon his mother, still grieving the loss of her husband, became overwhelmed by Lawrence's behavior and, for the safety of her daughter, she had Lawrence placed at a state institution for the mentally and emotionally disturbed.

The institution was housed in a beautiful gothic-style building, surrounded by giant old trees and rolling rural hills. But life inside institutions was hard, and Lawrence was subjected to many forms of "treatment" that today would disturb most of us to even think about.

Lawrence spent twenty-six years in the institution, and in his later years, when asked about his time there, he would respond with a resounding, "They can all go to hell!"

By the 1970s, hundreds of thousands of Americans were being held involuntarily in state facilities for the mentally and emotionally disturbed, some of them for "crimes" as simple as being homeless. State hospitals had become overwhelmed with patients whose needs they weren't always equipped to meet, and many of these patients were subjected to abuse and neglect. The deinstitutionalization movement was sweeping the Western world, a call to release people from involuntary commitment and bring them back into their communities. It was this movement that finally set Lawrence free in 1972. After living nearly his entire life in an institution, he was let back into the world with little more than the clothes on his back.

Deinstitutionalization was a complicated process. The community-based mental health system was still in its infancy, and many of the people who were released were not provided the supports they needed to survive on their own. But for Lawrence, it was liberation. He moved to Rochester and found a job working in the laundry room at the Holiday Inn. He rented a small studio apartment on Prince Street and took great pride in his home. Despite the abuse and neglect it is now known was suffered by many of the patients at the state institution, Lawrence seemed to come out of the experience intact.

Lawrence was terminated from the Holiday Inn in 1977 but never explained the reasons. Lawrence was careful with his money and so he was able to live off his savings until he eventually qualified for public assistance.

Lawrence kept a clean house and took pride in being orderly with his record keeping and personal belongings. He was well groomed and quite capable of maintaining his personal hygiene. He prepared his meals and did his own shopping. Often he would come to Dimitri House for Afternoon Drop-In: a program that offers hospitality, something to eat, and a comfortable and safe place to spend the afternoon. He engaged in conversation with the volunteers and staff. Sometimes he would talk about his childhood before his father died. He never quite got over it. Dimitri House was like family to him and most times he was the last to leave, needing to share just one more story.

The time came when Lawrence was unable to live alone. Aging and health issues became a concern and a decision was made by his caseworker that he would move to a nursing home. He was only there for a short time—less than a month—and he died. Lawrence was eighty years old. Karen, a devoted friend, called to tell me the news. The wake would be the following day. There was no question, I would attend.

There were just four of us there to say goodbye to Lawrence. We sat silent for a while, kind of huddled in a semi-circle and then, one by one, we each began to share our favorite memory of Lawrence. My memory came to mind immediately. Lawrence told me this story several years ago and it has stayed with me. It went something like this:

"I'll never forget the Christmas right after my dad died of a heart attack, and he was only thirty-seven years old! All of a sudden, it was just me, my mom, and my little sister. It was hard for my mom because we didn't have that much money and Christmas was coming soon. I already knew it was gonna be an awful Christmas without my dad. I missed him so much. He showed me how to do lots of things that men need to know. My mom was sad and cried all the time. For past Christmases, she always made a bunch of Christmas cookies—all kinds—but not that year. I just knew we wouldn't have any presents either. We didn't even have a Christmas tree. Nothing was the same anymore. Christmas Eve came, but it sure didn't feel like it. I remember going to bed that night and I cried until I feel asleep.

"I woke up early on Christmas morning and headed downstairs for breakfast. When I walked into the living room, I could hardly believe my eyes. There in the middle of the living room was the thorn-apple tree from our side yard. My mom must have chopped it down and there it was in our living room, and it was all decorated! There was a chain made out of colored paper wrapped around the tree, and on each thorn was a big gumdrop. I couldn't believe it! It was the most beautiful Christmas tree I'd ever seen and I haven't seen a prettier one since."

When Lawrence told me that story, I could see that tree as clearly as if it was there in front of me, and for a few moments with his face aglow, he was that little boy forever preserved in a cherished memory.

GEORGE

MOST TIMES, WHEN I WOULD SEE A SHOPPING CART stashed behind the dumpster at Dimitri House, it was a sure bet that it belonged to George. It would be loaded with piles of scrap metal, bottles, microwaves, and sometimes even a kitchen sink! When I looked again, it would be gone.

For years, George lived on the street, the all-too-familiar life of one caught in the grip of addiction. Summers, winters, always pushing that cart to exchange his finds for cash to support his habit. Every now and then, he would stop in for lunch, or to ask for a pair of socks or a jar of peanut butter. He was a likable guy—very grateful, always polite.

He was missing for a while and then one day he stopped by the Afternoon Drop-In program just to say hi. I couldn't believe my eyes. He looked like a new man. He was all cleaned up: clean-shaven, new clothes, new shoes. It was good to see him looking so good. He had his own apartment now and was working at the Salvation Army. I asked if I could ask him something kind of personal. With a big smile on his face he said, "Sure."

"So how'd ya do it? How did you give up the drugs, George?"

He said, "Well, it's like this—I asked God to help me. Every morning I prayed to God to please help me and, one day, I woke up and I knew I was done and my life would be different. I was changed. No one can ever tell me that God doesn't answer prayers because I know He does and I'm the proof. I see my brothers out there still doing their thing and I know they want to know how I did it, but until they ask, they'll just have to wonder because really you gotta get it on your own —well, I mean with God's help. YOU have to ask."

It did my heart good to see George all cleaned up, but the part that really took my breath away was the light I saw in his eyes. He was finally living the life that he was meant to live and loving every minute of it.

SAM

OCCASIONALLY I STOP IN THE NIGHT SHELTER to see how things are going with the men. One particular evening as I was leaving, the doorbell rang. It was 11:00 p.m. It was Sam, a familiar guest, who comes to our drop-in program. He was with Coop, another guest. Coop told me he saw Sammy wandering around Main Street downtown and thought he needed to bring him to Dimitri House. I'll never know for sure, but I bet Coop had to do some convincing to get Sam to come with him because Sammy was really out of it.

Sam has an apartment so I couldn't imagine why he would be coming to Dimitri House at eleven at night. And his behavior seemed strange—he was quite restless. I invited him in to sit and chat. He put his head on the table and began to cry. "Something is wrong with me. I don't know what's wrong with me."

He seemed afraid and confused and he looked exhausted. I tried talking with him, but he wasn't making sense. I considered having him stay the night at Dimitri House. I would stay with him. But a little voice inside me said: "Call an ambulance."

He was hesitant about going to the hospital, but I told him I would follow in my car and stay with him until we knew what was going on.

When we arrived at the hospital, an aide took him in immediately. After doing the paperwork and answering some questions, I was told Sam had been there earlier in the day. I was surprised to hear that and asked why he had been released. A nurse told me, "Well, we see this a lot, you know. Had too much to drink. Wants to come in out of the cold . . ."

I tried to explain this was not the case. Sam doesn't drink or do drugs. He has an apartment and a place to stay. I went on further to say that I knew him and this wasn't like him. Something was wrong. I told them they needed to do some testing or X-rays or something.

They performed blood work and a physical exam but hesitated with further testing. I kept trying to convince the hospital staff that this was not normal behavior for Sam. The doctor finally gave in to my pleading and ordered a CT scan. His X-rays revealed a large blood clot in his brain. Emergency surgery was scheduled immediately. There was nothing more I could do.

I left for home around 2:00 a.m. My mind was racing. "It's a good thing I stopped in the shelter tonight!" . . . "Thank goodness Coop somehow got him to Dimitri House!" . . . "What if Sammy had stayed home?" What if this, what if that? I felt anger, relief, and gratitude all at the same time.

When I arrived home, it was 2:30. I collapsed on my bed and cried my eyes out. I knew that God's hand was on Sam that night and that I was witness to a miracle. Sam survived the surgery without complication. He is the same Sam.

Today he is the one Dimitri houseguest who is also a volunteer. He takes pride in helping out and thinks of it as his job. Sam knows he's welcome here, and that knowledge has kept him coming back for years.

DEBBIE

DEBBIE STRUGGLED WITH DRUG ADDICTION FOR YEARS. She supported her habit through prostitution and although she was in her mid-thirties, she acted very childlike. She often carried a stuffed animal and when she wore makeup, it looked like she was playing dress-up. Smudged lipstick, heavy eye shadow. She thought she looked beautiful though. And in her way, she did.

Recently out of rehab, she stopped by Dimitri House. I was opening the door for the afternoon program and she came running up the driveway. "Hi, Fran." She giggled. She had put on a little weight.

She threw her arms around me and gave me a big hug. "Did you miss me?"

I responded with a resonant "YES!" It really was so good to see her.

Her afternoon was spent playing UNO, her favorite card game, and catching up with some of her friends, volunteers, and staff. Debbie was so childlike and everybody loved her.

When time came to close up for the afternoon, I noticed her eyeing a stuffed animal rabbit tucked between two books on the bookshelf. With a twinkle in her eye, she asked, "Hey, where did you get that cute bunny?"

I just smiled and handed it to her. She hugged it tight and held it like a baby. "Thanks, Fran! You know how I am." And she took off skipping down the driveway.

JAKE

ABOUT TEN YEARS AGO, IN THE GRIP OF A HEROIN addiction, Jake shared a needle with a man who had AIDS. The rest is history.

Jake came into the food cupboard this week. He wasn't looking so good. I asked him how he was doing and he told me he was getting tired. He leaned toward me and whispered, "Can I tell you something? I've stopped taking my meds. You know—for the virus. I fought hard, Fran, you know I did, but I'm tired. I'm ready and I want to go home. I have a death wish. I want to die on my birthday. It's the day I came into this world and it's the day I want to go out."

I told Jake, "No matter what, we're here for you."

His eyes filled with tears and he held on to me for a few moments. When he let go, he was smiling and said I reminded him of his sister.

I told him, "Jake, I am your sister."

Several weeks later, again at our afternoon program, Jake stopped in for lunch. Actually I was quite surprised to see him. I thought for sure that the end had come for Jake, but there he was in living color with a big smile and a hug. "Thanks for being there for me a couple weeks back—it was a bad day and I was actually thinking of taking myself out, but every time I closed my eyes, I kept hearing you say, 'No matter what, we're here for you' and I hung on to that. I'm back on track and I'm not gonna let the devil take me down! I'm gonna fight and I'm gonna live!"

Jake is still living and occasionally comes by to say hi. He even goes into juvenile correction facilities and high schools to tell his story during school assemblies. He's not happy about living with the virus, but he says, "Franny, if I can save one kid, then it's all been worth it."

ELLEN

ELLEN WAS A YOUNG WOMAN finally able to see her son again after having been in jail for some time. She had six years clean, but as often happens, life threw her a curveball, she couldn't handle it, and she relapsed and landed in jail. But she loved her son and was doing everything she could to stay on track to get her boy back permanently. She'd say, "My little boy—he's my heart."

We would sit on the stairs to my office and she would just sob and constantly say, "I'm so sorry for crying." I could never know exactly what Ellen was experiencing, but when my sons were little babies they would go to their father's every other weekend and the separation almost killed me. She was a mother missing her child.

She stopped by recently to ask if she could use our washer. Her son was coming for a weekend visit and she wanted him to have fresh sheets on his bed and clean clothes. She wanted things to be perfect for him. When she finished her laundry, she came into my office to thank me. "I want my son to know that I can be a good mom. I want him to come back home."

TOM

TOM HAS A PROBLEM WITH ANGER. He's a veteran and he says he hates everybody. Well, not everybody, and he gives me a wink. He can't concentrate, he has back pain, and he likes getting high. I offer him a suggestion that maybe he needs something to do to keep his mind occupied. He tells me he likes Paint-by-Number. We head off to a craft store.

After wandering through the aisles, he chooses a Paint-By-Number Kit called A Tribute to the Veterans of the Vietnam War. He starts describing how he will add his own touch: a blending of blues here and these grays a little darker and so on. I can see it only when he has finished it.

On the way back to Dimitri House, I drop him off at the library and later on that afternoon he appears at the door with a small bouquet of hyacinths and daffodils.

"Here," he says, "It was nice what you did for me."

ALEJÁNDRO

ALEJÁNDRO WAS ONE OF OUR SHELTER GUESTS. One afternoon he came in to tell me that he got a job. He was really excited because he hoped that soon he would be able to get his own place. There was just one catch: he needed work clothes. The required uniform was black boots, a light blue shirt, and dark pants.

I was able to get him almost all the items from a secondhand store that gives away gently used clothing for people in need. However, the boots were a different story. He had HUGE feet and I couldn't find gently used boots anywhere, let alone a size fourteen!

I jumped in my car and headed for the nearest shoe store, a Payless. They actually had two pairs of size fourteen boots: one in beige and one in black. I said, "I'll take the black pair."

I arrived back at Dimitri House just about closing time and handed him the boots. He was shocked. Brand new boots, and his size! When he put them on, I noticed his socks looked like Swiss cheese, so I gave him six pairs of brand new socks.

The next day, after he had a morning of training, he arrived at our drop-in program for lunch wearing his work uniform. The look of pride—not only on his face but in the way he stood so tall and confident—was a sight to behold. He came over to me, kissed me on the cheek, and told me his life was better because of Dimitri House.

BRAD

BRAD IS A CHALLENGE, TO SAY THE LEAST. He's an "in your personal space" kind of guy, probably due to untreated mental illness and an addiction to crack. He has an apartment—or most likely a room he calls home—and he rides a bike to wherever he needs to go.

Brad is very respectful, though, in spite of a tough street-life. I don't know much about his growing up years, but he was surely raised by good people who taught him manners. When he needs or wants something, it's always please and thank you.

He stops by a lot to ask for gloves, socks, or hygiene products, and he receives food from our emergency food cupboard once a month. One particular day, while picking up his food, a donation of some wonderful pastries arrived. I gave him a choice of which ones he would like best. He pointed to his favorite: chocolate éclairs, and his face filled with true delight. He stepped back, gave a small bow and said, "My dear sweet lady, for your kind gesture, please consider yourself kissed!"

He hung his bags of food on his handlebars, hopped on his bike, and away he went, singing all the way.

JOHN

ONE OF OUR SHELTER GUESTS had gotten into the habit of arriving late every Friday night for shelter. The cut-off time is 10:00 p.m. and he would call about 9:30 to say he'd be late because he was working. If a shelter guest is arriving late for shelter, he is required to show a statement from his employer. However John never provided one. This routine went on for about four weeks so I asked the volunteers to call me if he showed up late again. Rules are rules.

The very next Friday night, one of the volunteers called me at 11:00 to say that John had arrived late again. I wasn't going to budge—like I said, rules are rules—until John asked if he could speak with me. A shaky voice began to explain, "Please, Fran, I was embarrassed to tell my employer that I was homeless and staying in a shelter. Can you please give me another chance? I'm trying to get back on my feet and I can almost afford my own place now. I've been saving my paychecks. Please?"

How could I say no? Would I give up on my kids? What if one of my sons was asking me for another chance? How many millions of second chances had God given me?

There but for the grace of God go I . . .

FRED

FRED STAYED IN OUR SHELTER for about five years. He'd had a good job, but after the death of his wife, he suffered a serious nervous breakdown. Unable to cope with his deep loss, he was let go from his job. Eventually he lost his home and his car and found himself homeless at the age of sixty.

Recently he was able to begin collecting social security. Since then, every two to three months, Dimitri House receives a donation from Fred with a note attached:

NO NEED TO THANK ME—
YOU HAVE ALREADY DONE ENOUGH.

CHARLIE

OFTEN ON MY LUNCH HOUR, I walk down to midtown. The fresh air does me good and it's a nice break before opening up for the afternoon program. Many times, I'll bump into one of the regulars from Dimitri House. We might chat for a bit and then I continue on my way.

One man who I see often is a sweet little guy named Charlie. He's been on the street nearly thirty-five years as a result of drugs. He makes his money by dolling up cars. He works right on Main Street cleaning them inside and out until they look sparkling new.

He usually spots me first and I'll hear, "Hey you" and when I look his way, he'll give me one of his beautiful, toothless smiles.

I bumped into him during Christmastime, only this time I spotted him first. This time there was no "Hey you," no smile. This time it was a sad, lonely pair of eyes looking back at me. He didn't have gloves on, his nose was running and his feet looked wet and frozen.

We talked for a while and he was holding back the tears. He told me how he never much looked forward to Christmas. "You see, my mother died on a very precious holiday. Christmas Day. I don't know why, but this Christmas is just killing me."

I asked him back to Dimitri House for the afternoon. We walked back together in silence. I fixed him a plate of food and brought him upstairs. I took off his soaked sneakers and socks

21

and let him soak his feet in a tub of warm water. His whole body relaxed and he started to talk. He shared some beautiful memories of his mother. He told me she always told him, "Charles, now, I know you my boy, but you as good as anybody and don't you never forget it."

Dolores

I remember seeing Dolores the first time and wondering, "What's her story?" Most times she was with Jimmy, her husband, but I never got the impression she was all that happy. She would walk up the driveway a few feet behind him, like she wasn't worth it or something. But there was beauty in her face.

So many who come to Dimitri House have said they feel invisible. "People like us don't matter. They look through us like we're not even here."

What must that feel like? Not to be noticed? Not to matter?

When opening the doors for our afternoon program, I saw Dolores hurrying up the driveway to come in. I greeted her by name. "Hi, Dolores—how are you?"

She looked at me with a surprised expression on her face. "You said my name? I like that! You know my name!"

She spent that afternoon at Dimitri House, chatting with the other guests, laughing and having a good time. I spotted her every now and then, and it was clear that she was in a place she felt she belonged. And she did.

CECIL

CECIL COMES TO OUR FOOD CUPBOARD regularly. The last time he was here, he was moving about rather slowly and was clearly uncomfortable. I asked him if he was okay and he proceeded to tell me he had a serious hernia but couldn't have the surgery until he received Medicaid approval. Medicaid was dragging its feet and he was getting depressed.

He explained how the other day, while in a grocery store, he was accused of shoplifting because a security officer saw the bulge in his lower left abdomen and thought he had stuffed something in his pants. He had to show the security officer his hernia.

He thought that was terrible. I told him it was terrible *and* demoralizing. As he continued with his story, he started to laugh at the ridiculousness of it and then I started to laugh and together we laughed for a good five minutes.

"Thank God for this place," he said. "No matter what's going on in my life, I always feel better when I come to Dimitri House."

RICKY

RICKY WAS A GENTLE MAN: always polite, always respectful, and so very thoughtful. Before leaving after lunch at Dimitri House, he would pop his head in the kitchen to thank the volunteers and staff for the wonderful meal.

He loved nature and appreciated the animals and the flowers and the trees. It wasn't unusual for him to appear at the door with a bunch of flowers, probably from someone's garden. He loved to feed the birds and was often seen downtown surrounded by birds nibbling little morsels of stale bread.

Although he had distanced himself from his family, he shared tender memories of his sisters and brother. His step-father was always "Dad" and he cherished his mother, Dorothy. He couldn't talk about her without crying.

Ricky was a friend to all, sharing what he had whether it was food, clothes, or booze.

And Ricky was a storyteller, right down to every last detail. He talked of his childhood with fondness: the house on Brighton Street, the magnolias in the side yard, the adventures of being a Boy Scout. He talked of his poetry, and his talent was revealed the day he presented a poem just for me.

Ricky also had a gift for making people laugh. The day I took him to the hospital, I had to leave his room several times because I was laughing so hard. I think the nurse thought we were both a bit nutty. When she asked Ricky about any illnesses, his response was, "Well, there's been some diarrhea—it runs in the family."

I asked Ricky how he felt about dying. He said, "I really wanted to be here longer because I wanted to do more."

Then I asked him if he was afraid.

"No. It was good here and I know it will be good there."

MARK

THE HOMELESS ARE A CLOSE-KNIT COMMUNITY and many have street names. Mark's street name was Bear and that's the name he preferred.

I didn't know Bear all that well. He wasn't a regular at Dimitri House, and the times he stopped by he came and went in a dash. He was an alcoholic and drinking had cruelly taken over his life, his being, his soul. However, there was something very sweet about him. I wish I had known him better. Bear died a few days ago.

Walking into a funeral home to pay respect for "one of our people" is familiar to me, but it's never easy. The homeless don't live very long. Lives are cut short because of drug addiction, alcoholism, lack of healthcare, or untreated mental illness. But still, when one's life is over, it must be honored.

I was directed into the chapel by the funeral director where a handful of people were talking quietly. The casket was open. Bear looked peaceful. They don't always, but he did. He had on a black leather vest, a t-shirt, and jeans. A glittery cross was around his neck. Bear would have been proud of just how good he looked.

I said a little prayer and decided to sit for a while. A woman approached me to ask who I was. I told her I was Fran from Dimitri House. She smiled. Her name was Kathy and she sat down next to me and began to talk. She was Bear's girlfriend. She shared stories of their twenty-five years together: the good times and the bad. She laughed and cried.

She thanked me for coming.

Needing to get back to the afternoon program at Dimitri House, I approached the casket one last time to say goodbye. A display of pictures had just arrived: Bear in second grade . . . at a party as a teenager . . . with family at Christmas . . . playing ball in a park.

A life. A life to be honored.

BILL

BILL STAYED IN OUR WINTER SHELTER for about five years. He always chose the same bed: it was Bill's bed! He was easy to get along with, not a drinker, never touched a drug or even a cigarette. Bill was homeless because of severe mental illness. He had schizophrenia.

Born in Elmira, Bill had a fairly normal life growing up. He had great parents and three sisters. He married his high school sweetheart, Marion, and the first several years of their marriage were spent happily raising their children, working hard, and living a good life. But that was not to be.

Bill began to show signs of strange behavior and withdrawal. He had little to do with his children and began to experience fits of violence toward them and Marion. Somewhere in his clouded mind though, he must have known that it was best to leave his family for the fear of what could happen. He eventually ended up in Rochester.

A neighborhood man who owned some apartments hired Bill to do odd jobs and that's how he supported himself for years. During the summer months he would be seen mowing, repairing, cleaning, painting—Bill did it all. But in the winter months, when work was scarce, he would spend the cold months at Dimitri House.

Several shelter volunteers began to be concerned about Bill's coughing during the night. After several weeks, he was told he must see a doctor, much to his resistance. The coughing was keeping the other guests awake and there was real concern for Bill's health. After a few visits to the hospital, Bill was diagnosed with Stage IV lung cancer.

A treatment plan was presented and Bill agreed. He was a real trouper: never complaining, remaining very hopeful. Until permanent housing could be established, the volunteers and staff stayed with him day and night at Dimitri House. He spent his evenings watching TV upstairs. At the time, the Winter Olympics were going on and he was captivated by the figure skating. He would get so excited and involved watching it night after night.

Dimitri volunteers took him to his treatment appointments and he was beginning to accept the love and care being showered on him. We were working with a social worker who eventually found permanent housing for Bill at Cornerstone, a facility for the mentally ill and disabled. Not a very cheery place, so when Bill was feeling well enough, I would pick him up and bring him to the Afternoon Drop-In Program. He loved playing cards with the other guests, but sometimes he would just sit and watch.

On the way back to Cornerstone, it seems I would consistently hit the same bump in the road. I'd wince and then apologize, concerned about Bill's discomfort. It became a joke between us and he would make wisecracks as we approached that darn bump and sure enough, I'd hit it!

Time was running out for Bill and he asked if he could see the priest at Corpus Christi Church. A meeting was arranged and they spent about twenty minutes in private conversation. When I took Bill back to Cornerstone that day, his exact words were, "Well, that was a load off my mind." That's all he said, but he sure looked lighter after that meeting.

Bill had a chance to see his sisters and a couple of his children toward the end, but I'm not sure he appreciated it like we thought he would. It seemed to take him back to a dark place and he told us he didn't want to see any of them again.

It was getting more difficult for Bill to come to Dimitri House for the afternoons. His energy was fading and his interest was gone. Arrangements were made for Bill to go into

Isaiah House, a hospice in the neighborhood. They wanted to transport him by ambulance, but Bill said, "Oh I think I can get in Frannie's little blue car—she'll get me there." And I did.

When we arrived at Isaiah House, everything was ready for him. His bed linens were turned down; a lamp in the corner of the room glowed a soft light. A bouquet of flowers freshly picked from the garden adorned the mantle. The whole atmosphere exuded a sense of peace and safety. I left the room while the volunteers helped Bill undress and get into bed, and when I came back in to see how things were moving along, Bill was sleeping soundly.

Death was drawing nearer and Bill was struggling. His eyes stayed open for days as he lay still, except for his breathing. The lapses between each breath were further and further apart.

"Is he gone?"

And then another breath.

The hours of labored breathing seemed to go on forever and then—silence. So still. So quiet. It was as if the whole world stopped for just a moment.

Bill's life was over. He was gone. A life lived the best way he knew how.

JOYCE

JOYCE WAS A DEAR WOMAN. She had been coming to Dimitri
House for years. Unless she really needed it, she never asked
for one thing. Her apartment was a humble dwelling, furnished
with things from here and there. If she knew of someone who
was homeless, she'd open her door without question, sharing
what little she had and many times jeopardizing her own safety.

Joyce lived next door to Dimitri House. I saw her just
about every day in her travels. She would be heading to
Midtown or returning and I would hear her all-too-familiar
voice, "Hi, Fran! Hi . . . hi!" And she would be waving her
arms way up in the air. "Have a nice day!"

She had such a simple way about her. When the nice
weather arrived and flowers were in bloom, she'd fix her hair
up in a little bun embellished with a lilac or a rose. She liked
jewelry and scarfs and had a way of wearing them just so. She
appreciated her femininity and enjoyed being a woman.

Joyce had a deep faith. She would say, "Just ask Jesus. He
loves you and will take care of you. And then ask Him for
Heaven."

After attending a Sunday morning church service, on her
way to a lunch program, Joyce collapsed on the street and died
from a massive heart attack.

Joyce's family had a wake for her. I had thought we were
her only family, and it seems while she was alive—we really
were. But Joyce had a sister who lived right here in Rochester.
And her daughter, who she had not seen in over thirty years,

came in from Pennsylvania.

I spoke at Joyce's funeral. I asked everyone to close their eyes, and I said, "Picture Joyce as you last saw her. Whether it was three days ago or thirty years ago."

I closed my eyes and I could hear Joyce saying, "God says we need to take care of each other."

ALICIA

I SAT IN THE CORNER OF THE FAINTLY LIT ROOM, silent, as I watched the hospice staff clean Alicia's body to prepare it for the undertaker. They took care to cover each part respectfully as they gently moved down her body. Moments before, I held her hand and told her it was okay to go. It was my birthday and the thought of Alicia dying on my birthday was dreadful, but I soon realized that it was a beautiful gift. Death, like birth, is a holy moment.

I thought back to a day two years ago when Alicia came to Drop-In one afternoon to tell me that her HIV status had worsened. Alicia had led the dangerous lifestyle of prostitution and drugs and she was living with serious consequences. Visibly upset, she began to share her dreams that most likely would never come true.

"I wanted to marry Brian and have a fairy tale wedding," she cried, wiping her eyes.

I asked her where Brian was and she pointed him out from across the room. I motioned for him to come over and I asked him if he loved Alicia.

"Yes," he said, smiling.

I then asked him if he wanted to marry her.

"Yes," he said with an even bigger smile.

"Well," I said, "then let's have a wedding."

In one short week, the staff and volunteers at Dimitri House planned a wedding. I took Alicia shopping for a wedding dress at the Vietnam Veteran's second-hand store. There was just one wedding dress and one might have thought it was made for Alicia. It was a perfect fit. My sister fashioned a beautiful headpiece and veil and created a nosegay: pink and red, at Alicia's request. A cake was ordered, programs were printed, candy kisses were wrapped in netting with a tag: CONGRATULATIONS ALICIA AND BRIAN.

A minister was summoned to meet with Alicia and Brian to confirm their intentions. Preparations were underway.

Wedding day arrived. The dining room at Dimitri House had been transformed into a wedding chapel of pink fluff. One of our volunteers would give her away, another would do her hair and makeup, another would take pictures. The kitchen staff would prepare a reception meal. Another volunteer would play the wedding march on his keyboard. The moment was here.

The lights dimmed, the candles were lit, and the music began. Alicia descended the stairs and entered the room. She looked absolutely beautiful. Every bit the blushing bride. She took Brian's arm and the minister began. We all watched on as Alicia and Brian exchanged vows and their marriage was sealed with a kiss.

They walked a long red carpet to a waiting limousine.

Alicia's dream had come true, if just for one day.

DIMITRI

DIMITRI HOUSE IS NAMED AFTER DIMITRI MAMCZUR, a homeless man who lived in two taped-together cardboard boxes under an expressway bridge on I-590 in Rochester, New York.

On a cold, rainy November night in 1985 while heading back to his humble shelter, Dimitri was hit by a car. For two weeks the priest at Corpus Christi Church spent time with him. He anointed him and offered him gentle, encouraging words of hope. Dimitri died two weeks later.

Over 150 people came to Dimitri's funeral to say goodbye and celebrate his life. People who knew him shared stories about how he would help local merchants but decline money when offered, how he would give his last cigarette to a homeless friend, and how he would collect bottles and cans to buy bread to feed the birds.

Many were touched by Dimitri's story and made a commitment to do more for the homeless and poor of Rochester. From there, property was purchased and named Dimitri House.

Today, Dimitri House continues to honor Dimitri by serving its neighbors in need with love and acceptance, joining them on their journey.

ABOUT THE AUTHOR

Fran Morse worked at Dimitri House for nearly twenty-five years and believes it was her life's calling. Fran loves to garden and bike. Fran has two grown sons and three grandchildren. She lives in Rochester, New York with her dog, Jessie Mae.